Muscle Tree

MUSCLE TREE

BARBARA PARCHIM

Muscle Tree
Copyright © 2024 Barbara Parchim

First Flowstone Press Edition • September 2024
ISBN 978-1-945824-66-1

Author photo (back cover) by Kate Campbell
All other photos by Barbara Parchim

Flowstone Press,
an Imprint of Left Fork

www.leftforkbooks.com

Contents

1

winesap	3
story in the stone	5
duff	7
forgiving the marauders	8
holding space	9
reliquary	11
muscle tree	12
madrone berries	13
winter grace	15
twilight song	17

2

cypher	21
cypress bluff	23
from the sea	24
cephalopod	25
extinction	26
waking	28
reading the stars	29
an exuberant shout	30
indian sands	31
tundra light	33

3

cantabile	37
choir practice	39
ode to old uprights	41
anything you want	43
her metamorphosis	45
night moths	47
retriever	49
shapeshifting	51
feral	53
a thousand goodbyes	55
turtle pond	57
crossroads	58
canoeing on Lake Earl	59
dreamscape	61
haiku for hummers	62
fly me to the moon	63

4

exclusion zone	67
fisher	69
P-22	70
forest elk	71
improving the view	72
descent	74
telling the bees	75
the verge	76
sharp-shinned	78
the healer's hands	79
sparing the mandrake	80
chrysalis	82

1

winesap

after picking apples for 6 to 8 weeks
my ladder and I are close partners
rungs and rails smoothed from use
uncounted trips up and down

it's my last day of the season
and the grower
drives the forklift over to a secluded corner –
grass unkempt, trees scattered and very old

I lay the ladder in the grass
and climb the tree in front of me
broad horizontal limbs
fruit large and streaked – a Winesap

he relaxes in his seat,
the pressure of harvest behind him,
hands hanging slack as he talks
about the century old trees here

varieties that no one wants anymore –
fallen out of favor –
not commercially viable
like the Red delicious, Jonathans or Romes

I am clambering in the tree, listening
as he speaks, the eyes,
bluer than Indian summer sky, soften,
the features relax

more talking than he's done all season –
imagining before his time
and before his father's time
when this tree was young

and it's then that I see it –
this is love –
unreasonable, illogical and unprofitable –
the best kind

this matriarch will stand with all the others
until she can't –
age will take her,
not the saw

story in the stone

clearing the channel downhill from the spring
I found the grinding stone
half buried in the bank –
small enough for a child's lap

the depression, too shallow for grinding acorns,
wore a rime of color,
maybe residue of manzanita berries, chokecherries
or camas roots mixed with deer fat

the stone left behind by the acorn people
when the strange travelers came
with their wagons and tired horses
their noise and their papers claiming the land

the stone left behind
near the carefully tended camas swale,
the plank house under sheltering alders,
the willow bundles still soaking in the creek

left behind
in the company of centuries-old oaks
still weighted with the year's acorn harvest
heavy with promise

the acorn people thinking
maybe they could return
when the circle of seasons came around again
as it had always been

the stone sits in my flower bed now,
between the sage and roses
gathering sunlight and dust
and then moonlight and rain,
the rime darkening with moisture –
the sweet relief of water

in our exodus, whenever it comes,
our eviction will be of our own design –
the sum of our excesses and failures
left behind in the fire and ash,
while under the too too hot sun
the stone endures

duff

the word belies the complexity –
layers of cushioned softness
we take for granted
between earth's mineral layer
and our footfall

what we miss walking –
leaf and needle
centipede and millipede
beetle and salamander
mosses and mycelium

upright creatures –
we move forward-facing
listening for bird call or twig snap
or crane our necks upward
to watch crows wheeling in canopy

but on hands and knees
gently sift any square foot
and count the hundreds of lives
hidden in this darkest layer

all of life teems here –
birth, proliferation, death

this is the past
this is the future –
breath beneath our feet

forgiving the marauders
—for Kate

the mason bee house
is being invaded by parasitic wasps

I worry and fret about the bees –
but she says only "let them be"

standing barefoot and Rubenesque
in her overalls and loose shirt

ruddy and a little sweaty from working
her hair a mop of dishevelment

there is an undercurrent of buzzing around her
as she explains in a sweet high voice

the purpose and beauty of these marauders –
their habits and peculiarities

sighing, she wonders where it gets her –
a life working in gardens,

bare feet and hands that ache,
studying and nurturing these native wasps

but nevertheless, she insists –
we don't pull the purslane when weeding

the wasps are a cloud
laying their eggs on the fleshy leaves

I bear witness to this – their urgency –
learning a language of shorter lives

holding space

the orchard out the kitchen window is dormant
but first color soon will be the crocuses
between the Gravenstein and the clothesline

marking plots in our small family cemetery
grown larger over these 50 years –
a scatter of four cats and eight dogs

a patch of purple asters over one
another with a cracked mosaic
that loses pieces every frosty winter

most not inscribed, despite best intentions –
I opted for crocus bulbs instead –
so that now I need a map

to keep track of who's who
in a wild patch of flat stones
and Russian knapweed

hands in soapy water –
remembering lives that always ran too short
departures that surrendered us to grief

moonlight patterns the sheltering ground,
the wind soughs orchard branches
and stirs small blue, purple and yellow blooms

the crocuses are silently holding space –
a long pause before the rest of spring advances,
this annual quiet reminder

before spent fruit tree blossoms
carpet the ground – a fragrant shroud
and the crocuses return to sleep

reliquary

the old oak with outstretched arms
was splitting in two
after standing for 2 or 3 centuries

pocked with acorn woodpecker granaries
and nest holes like avian graffiti,
one leafless limb hung over the road
and would need to come off to save the tree

we salvaged an abandoned nest
attached to some mistletoe stems
at the cragged elbow of the limb,
woven by a western kingbird
of lichen, horsehair,
orange baling twine and white knitting yarn

a row of fledges and parents
perched on the phone line watching –
butter yellow and dove grey –
hawking for insects in the summer heat
and sputtering their staccato calls

the nest now hangs on my porch,
an avian artifact by a master weaver,
a delicate pouch lined with down and felt –
reliquary for the memory of eggs

muscle tree

the madrone near the top of the ridge –
slightly bent – spirals to the forest canopy
gathering her share of sun and wind

we call her the muscle tree
her orange, winding, sinuous trunk
shining in spring rain

running our hands over her smooth trunk –
her skin, like ours,
wants to be touched

neither supple muscle of a lover's arms
nor water-sculpted canyon slickrock,
but something in between – sentient, yet other

she is kin enough
to break us open
and spill our tenderness

madrone berries

robins on a December morning
at the edge of the woods

a cacophony – hundreds, maybe thousands –
pausing their migration this whole month

to forage a heavy crop of madrone berries –
colors of orange and ash, raucous and jostling

incessant chattering of *tuks* and *peeks,*
like opening my door into an aviary with no walls

when silence suddenly falls, I scan for hawks –
the coopers slicing low through the trees

or the red-shouldered flying overhead –
before the feeding frenzy resumes

I collect a few berries – an imperative sent by the birds

imagining myself in an earlier time
with basket and crimson-stained fingers

I scan the world at my feet with a different set of eyes

berries – the missed ones –litter the forest floor,
amongst fallen leaves, deer droppings and fungi

sitting by the fire, I string berries
for two evenings – a mindless meditation

when 18 inches of snow fall over two days,
the woods are hushed with a mantle of snow

the next day, snowmelt fills the upper ditch,
robins bathe and chatter, stabbing for worms

the morning finally comes when I open the door
and the woods are quiet – almost bereft

seven long strands of madrone berries
hang by the wood stove – nature's mala beads

winter grace

the spring stopped flowing this summer
for the first time in 46 years

I hung a ribbon
from the lower limb of a seedling plum tree
that overlooks the source –
a small invocation –
and then set out the galvanized tub
to fill with water

evenings, I watched from the front porch –
the deer were fearful,
until thirst made them brave

in the weeks and months of relentless heat
red dragonflies – meadowhawks –
would obelisk in the sun to reduce exposure
as they waited for prey

the season became one to endure –
and I whispered of winter grace
to the parched garden paths
wondering when the well would run dry

now I smell the promise of bare white beauty
on the breath of ancient trees

a raven soars over a rising forest mist,
as ducks fly in v's overhead
earth's body of sea and rock beneath my feet,
mountains shift gray and white with soft light

it feels like more than hope
in the golds, yellows and reds of autumn –
winter's respite will fit
like a mantle of snow on the mountain
the spring will sigh when she reawakens
and her flow will mirror the moon

twilight song

after the shovels are cleaned and put away
but before the deer come down out of the woods to browse
after the wind has died down in the orchard
but before the horizon in the west loses hue
after the dragonflies are done hawking for insects
but before the bats have come out of their daytime niches
the wren is singing his song of the evening in the willows
singing his heart out in the pause between day and night
the moment when you might take those few minutes
in the rocker on the porch and take your boots off
when the quiet almost makes the air thicker
when there is still a possibility the world might be all right
this is the thing you will remember
when you're ready let go of wakefulness

2

cypher

the aurora borealis this first time
begins as the loons are yodeling crazily
from the far shore across the lake,
not yet frozen in this northern winter

it appears as a luminous semicircle
stretching the entire horizon,
like a giant planet gone off course,
ready to collide with earth

as it grows and looms closer,
we huddle on the pier,
caught between fear and fascination
as I keep asking – what is it? –
until the edges begin breaking up,
lazy streamers of green, blue and purple
veils shifting and shrouding –
slow motion, exquisite and impossible,
across the palette of northern sky

too soon the sky returns to constellations,
the loons settle for the night
and adrenaline slows in the arteries –
the mystery solved, but not yet ordinary

*

another nugget of clarity to join the others –
small enough to fit in the pocket
and pull out when the evening news
proves too much to face yet again

something shiny a crow would stash –
a prism turning in the sun,
a crystal found half-buried in the sand,
a bit of gold chain glinting at the garden gate,
or this half-hour of ethereal lights
like some cosmic cypher
hovering over our wounded planet –
fragile, after all, but not yet lost

cypress bluff

ancient cypress and shore pine live here –
passing by, convoluted seedpods crunch underfoot
like wrinkled marbles

the land calls to me with every visit –
wind-sculpted forest, a sheltered creek,
the bluff overlooking the sea and the river

I enter the realm of the impossible
and call it my land –
the English daisies run rampant in the grass

the bluff, high enough to evade the next tsunami,
hovers and sighs with old watchful eyes
that have already seen everything

storms, rough seas, relentless wind,
the old lighthouse before it was shuttered,
the foghorn before the complaints about noise

wise and twisted leaning trees,
have seen the house I built
in the ether of my dreams

gray-shingled, infused with salt and saudade,
the wide porch holds scavenged driftwood –
shell fossils and agates along the railing

already comfortably worn and shabby,
it waits as if abandoned –
though it has never been inhabited

from the sea
(on seeing the Peter Iredale)

she rests on the shore – huge –
jutting out of the sand
like a fantastical sculpture

or a dark-boned carcass
nothing left but iron hull
and remnants of the masts pocked with rust

almost buried, these masts are
uncanny now at eye level –
odd patterns surround them in the sand

symmetrical encryptions of another language,
as though something
still lives and breathes below

I touch the iron latticework of the hull
forged by other hands over 100 years ago
framing the surf once home to this barque

the skeletal hull beckons –
I hesitate to enter the looming sanctum –
as though at any moment

the ship will rouse and shudder,
like some long-slumbering beast,
to return home on the next retreating wave

cephalopod

my arm in the tank up to my elbow,
a sudden shock of cold and then
his tentacles are wrapping around my forearm –
each suction cup operating independently

an alien intimacy –
alarming at first, then oddly comforting,
like wearing a thunder shirt during a storm

gentle but firm, he explores –
he may know more about me
than I know about him

changing from a dull gray to a rosy hue
he is like a watery bloom –
Chinese flowering tea blossoming in a glass pot

this brief encounter in his small tank
may be his only enrichment today

9 brains, 500 million neurons,
and three hearts –
in case one breaks, are there two to spare?

the sea, only a block away,
is thrumming on the shore of the bay –
first heartbeat, first home

then, the sudden thought, his or mine:
all we need is 20 minutes and a bucket

extinction

the sea really is vermillion
certain times of the year

vaquita, I see you –
sleek and supple, fin slicing surf

almost the same size,
we are more alike than not –
warm-blooded, shy, panda-eyed

I came from the sea once
but have forgotten much

a mistake was made –
we flourished and became too many

took more than our share
began depleting our home

you may number 30
or possibly only 10 now

I want to hear your language
before it's extinguished forever

teach me –
we will speak of joy while we can

take me with you –
the sea will embrace us
our voices will join the others

her memory is long
and she will make room for us

I came from the sea once –
surely it won't be hard to return

I will leave my anguish behind –
a tattered robe on the shore

waking

there is light –
I can see it through the slits of my eyelids

quickly shutting them again
amorphous shapes writhe on the backs of my lids

pulsing and amniotic, I cling to this watery world
before consciousness fully takes hold

almost weightless – until I move,
and my body remembers gravity

they call it the crack of dawn, don't they?
silent, but relentless and insistent, nonetheless

time to rouse finally –
drinking coffee in bare feet on the front porch

I watch shadowy deer that have been up all night,
still browsing the last apple drops in the grass

we intersect here, in this moment
breathing the same air, watching the light change

dawn holds us in this tableau of stillness
before we remember we are different

reading the stars
—for Michael and Jaz

a glance that maybe lingered –
before submergence
for years or minutes
to wait for another season
another time
limbs trailing like kelp in the deep
until the clink of glass in the forge
until the whispering of the poet's pages
signaling surfacing, finally,
together

the sea slaps and then swells
beneath the hull of the boat
as they roll and tumble –
but they are good at this now
as a whale sighs nearby
in the darkest amethyst night,
they will stand on the deck
and read the stars –
a map of constellations –
and always know where they are

an exuberant shout

I stand on a shoreline outcrop
   of cluster anemones
   and imagine a flighted release

as the thing not imagined –
   my father's ashes –
   erupt from my hand

after a 10-year wait –
   like an exuberant shout
   over the frothing surf

and into the briny spray
   of the wind he loved
   while murres and gulls

hover and dive and congregate
   over the sea stacks they nest on
   and bray their mating calls onto shore

unwitting witnesses to this brief shade
   once come from stars and sea-born
   now returning

indian sands

laying back in the sun
on a bed of beach pea vine and sand verbena
we watched a group of pelicans
swoop low over the swells

as one of us said
if we found ourselves alone
we could be roommates again
and where would that be?

ah, but there was the stumbler –
I dislike southern California heat
and she dreaded southern Oregon winters,
so we just let the thread of what if's
sink into semi-somnolence

years later her husband did pass
before the rest of us –
a recurrence of a cancer long gone –
saying to me during a last phone call,
"of the four of us, if I go first, does that mean I win?"
gallows humor until the end

but by then the slow, relentless tsunami of Alzheimer's
had already begun its surge in her
and on a hot day in September,
six months later, finally crested

we didn't roll the dice or draw straws –
what were we thinking?
that we could rearrange the stars?
stop the tides or negotiate with the wind?

but we weren't thinking –
only in a slow drowse on a summer's day in June
soaking up each other's company
at the top of a sandy cliff
that could have collapsed into the ocean
if there was an earthquake

but it didn't and there wasn't
and we sat up then to watch the pelicans –
reversing course – and for a moment
we skimmed over a sea of possibilities

tundra light

hushed and serene
the light is everything here –
pink and gold and purple
falling on centuries-old lichens

ice on alpine tundra
tiny sparklers in the coldest sun
a white that blinds the eyes
until cloud and haze move in

harsh – this is a harsh
that the arctic hare, snowy owl,
muskox and arctic fox
were made for –

a harsh that guard hairs, tufted feet,
that down and thick fur protect against –
a harsh that the burrow and hibernation
provide respite and sanctuary from

when a frenzy of life begins
for 50-60 days in the summer
insects cloud the air
a madness of the briefest of lives

a flush of color on the landscape
as wildflowers race to flower and seed
before light diminishes
and life retreats underground

the mountains remain
stoic and timeless
overlooking their realm –
the certainty of this pulse of terrain

3

cantabile

I heard Beethoven's cantabile on the radio this morning
and remembered the image of him
laying his head on the piano to hear something –
anything – in the silence of his world

in the smoke and ashfall of yet another summer
I feel the anguish and exhaustion of hopelessness

wanting to lay my own head somewhere sheltered –
a bed of soft moss and moist needles
somewhere in a place where the earth feels safe
and the guilty reminder of our failures and excesses
is not a constant din like tinnitus in my ears

in the orchard I collect the apple drops in buckets,
toss them over the fence for the deer,
and clean the galvanized tub that holds their water
because too many drought years
stilled the spring that ran green and lush

trimming the pear limbs weighted with fruit
I carry on as though the wildfire were not
just a few miles away
humming the cantabile for our home as we wait

the lost settle as ash over the garden –
beloved forests and all their inhabitants
while the monarch I hoped to see all summer
sips nectar from the red valerian

immersed in this sweetness
unconcerned about what may remain tomorrow,
she continues what she knows best –
living her one irreplaceable life

choir practice

I practice singing *Peace is a'Come* in the car,
   visualize the world's collective masses –
   the children, the hunger

and as another log truck rolls out the dead
   from the mountain behind home
   I bargain with the universe –

if we bring peace to the people first....
   then can we save the forests?

I hum *Da pacem Domine* – give peace –
   the gravel road winding toward home,
   a slight crescendo and see the killing machines

like mutant malevolent storks,
   stretching their necks on the slopes –
   at rest after quitting time

machines that inhabited my childhood nightmares –
   chasing me down –
   are manifest now on this mountain

while the forest once alive with springs and creeks,
   serpentine meadows and bear dens,
   is now still in the unaccustomed emptiness

pileated woodpecker nests,
   salamanders and fungi, ponds and ferns,
   elderberries and wild grape

red shouldered hawk and raven roosts,
   all erased as though they never were
   while I harmonize *How Can I Keep from Singing*

I hear the earth – practiced at sacrifice –
   lifting her voice to join me, singing,
     how can I keep from weeping

ode to old uprights

I'm running up charcoaled stairs that crumble underfoot
in an old burnt-out house with no banister,
as workmen begin demolition with crowbars
oblivious to the piano huddled in a back room
desperately trying to plan an escape route –
I am caught in another *saving pianos* dream

    across the sea, someone is playing clair de lune
    for aging elephants at a sanctuary in Thailand
    the animals sway and shift gently on their feet
    ears waving in the breeze, a trunk tentatively caresses
    the top of the old upright –
    feeling the vibration

in Seattle, a homeless man plays on a street piano
at the outdoor market,
pounding out a tricky honkytonk riff
fingers running on muscle memory
in spite of his belongings in a heap
on the sidewalk beside him

    on Zillow, an old farmhouse is for sale,
    completely refurbished and empty of furnishings
    but for an old upright in the corner,
    too heavy to move, or left for a touch of shabby chic,
    it looks slightly out of place,
    like an old aunt sitting gingerly on a parlor chair

you can't even give away old uprights any more –
they decorate the sidelines at landfills and dumps,
missing keys, wood checked and warping in the rain,
a boxy perch for scavenging crows and ravens,
stoic and sad and lost all at once,
all of them with stories older than most of us

    I read someone salvaged the wood from three pianos
    abandoned at the dump,
    built a canoe of mahogany, cherry and oak
    and set it free on the water –
    now there are more stories to be told –
    listen – the river is humming another nocturne

anything you want

my mother said as we walked into the toy store
aisles lined with shelves of stuffed animals
of every shape and color

afraid of choosing the wrong one –
I looked for nothing too big
nothing too bright
but something to please her
on one of her rare visits

I worked so hard to be small and quiet
and so chose the littlest brown bear –
like me – small and quiet

*

"anything you want"
I said to my father on his 85th birthday
in the stones and crystals store

he chose a necklace –
a perfect piece of abalone shell
mounted in a teardrop silver setting

5 years later, after the diagnosis,
he handed it back to me –
never having taken it off

warm in my hand
I picked old man chest hair out of the chain

*

the bear sits in a woven basket now –
soft plush worn down to threadbare cotton –
the teardrop abalone around my neck
these consolations for the lost

her metamorphosis

there were signs early on –
as she compulsively folded, unfolded, refolded
jeans, t-shirts, underwear

meticulously filling the suitcase
then emptying it and starting over

spreading a micro-layer of blackberry jam
on her toast carefully

afraid to leave more than a faint wash of color –
as if what she loved most might be poison now

the inevitable losing, misplacing –
wallet, keys, phone, tickets, glasses

I was irritated and impatient –
she was being careless and scattered

then later, when we knew,
I felt guilty

my fingers circled her wrist as thin as a child's,
fragile bony stems connecting hand to arm

the scapulae on her back
protruded more with each visit

as though they'd rather be bird's wings –
as if they could fly away from confusion

what I remember most is hugging her –
scent of sage and roses in her hair

from our walk in the garden,
through the tidy gone rampant with neglect

afraid she would shatter in my arms,
like the finest Limoges china – unmendable

night moths

out the quiet doggie door
my arms full of schoolbooks,
I walk the long blocks near midnight
through darkened alleys and quiet streets

my friend waits with the car –
we toss our schoolbooks in back
and pumped with the adrenaline of risk
we drive to Chicago's near north side

the streets crowded with clubs,
the bouncers eye us warily
like soldier ants guarding against marauders

we are what we appear to be,
jailbait from the suburbs,
our presence a dare –
just another problem they don't need

giddy, we walk the seamy sidewalks
avoiding the drunk and despairing,
who look for cigarette butts or hope

we're not drinking, but drunk all the same
music spilling from doorways like pheromones –
the wail of a blues guitar
the bleating cat-call of a soprano sax

then, hovering at another open door,
we're caught by languid piano riffs
under the honeyed voice of Mose Allison –
seductive with the nectar of the forbidden

we forget the amorphous and fetid streets,
the cigarette smoke and cheap perfume,
and lean into the sound –
night moths drawn to the lily

retriever

heading out the door at the recess bell,
she skirts the playground bullies
through 12 inches of snow
and heads for the grove of hardwoods
at the back of the school property
her fingers stroke the fissured trunks
she has touched in greeting every day for weeks
but today, as snow falls in huge wet flakes,
in a goodbye caress

moving to the sloping bank,
thick with dried summer grasses under the snow
she falls back, cushioned and enclosed,
clasping her hands over her chest
no snow angels – just this cocooned quiet
the shrieks and laughter muffled now
from the shelter of her snow cave

soon her footprints will be buried,
and she will rest peacefully,
lost to the world until the spring thaw –
there will be no trace

warm and sleepy, she suddenly remembers the dog –
the dog that explores the creek with her
near the summer cabin on the lake,
happy to be off leash,
while she scouts for crawdads
redder than the rich iron ore soil
the dog that joins her at the end of the pier
listening to the night-time chorus of wolves
on the far shore of this remote lake

they carry each other's secrets –
the lucky rabbit's foot in her pocket,
the smuggled dog biscuit from the pantry –
her invisible hurts and his unexplained fears
he waits for her return and will be hungry

the bell rings signaling the end of recess
and still she remains, snow settling on her face,
just to feel what it would be like
but today, the dog, like the good retriever he is,
has changed everything

shapeshifting

I take the mask out of the box
   to keep the dust off its white feathers

won at a silent auction
   that, strangely, no one else bid for

a seeker's distillation of a vision quest,
   it vibrates with intention –

as though something animal wants to get out
   or invites me to come in

in truth, I want to wear it –
   feathers, silver beads and cowrie shells

and flee up the hill into the woods
   with the deer herd

leaving words and clothing behind
   suddenly swift and silent and sure

nostrils flared
   tasting the forest at the back of my throat

or catch the next breath of wind
   gusting through the cottonwood and alder

fly upslope to the glacial cirque
   and the aerie on the cliff face,

discolored from years of mutes –
    remnants of nest still tucked in a crevice

putting on the mask
    is stepping off the ledge –

becoming *other*....
    maybe becoming what I was meant to be

measuring risk and weighing consequences,
    the light changes at the edge of the woods

holding the mask, I feel a strange familiarity,
    an invitation to return to a place once known

feral

we spoke as strangers do
when they meet as travelers –
inconsequential and wary

we were there for the long cave tour –
darkened passageways,
hushed and slightly claustrophobic,
the guide speaking of
grizzly and jaguar bones
long at rest in the dark,
vaulted marble rock,
bats asleep in their ancestral home

returning to daylight,
snow a few inches deep on the ground,
the stranger opened the back of his car

there, another type of cave –
a bed covered in furs,
feathers and beads tied with rawhide
hanging from the sides

antlers and other bones at one corner,
a sheathed knife and small pieces of wood,
stones neatly cached in another,
the smell of cedar and sage

an arrangement – deliberate –
this diorama awash with ambient light

feral –
yet as compelling as the collections
of the bower bird
when attracting a mate

I was drawn as if to nest
but it was autumn verging on early winter –
better to den up for a long sleep
in this safe hibernaculum

daylight waned
as we stood in light snowfall,
hesitating, a question hung in the air,
before we stepped back,
each to return to our own lair

a thousand goodbyes
—for Carolyn

are lined up on the telephone wires
like all of summer's swallows
congregated for their migration south

one
two
three
I love you
bye

the ritual that made ending the calls easier –
alternating voices bridging the miles
always stretched between us

resting my head on the door frame
as I watch the deer below the garden
clean up apple drops and overgrown squash,
a California sister butterfly
lazily courses on the front porch,
bumping into the screen door
as though asking to come in

on any evening years ago
you'd be feeding the horses about now,
at the corrals near the rampant Matilija poppy,
dogs at your feet,
horses snorting, dusty and impatient

language had left you weeks ago –
exiting a back door in the synapses –
an English teacher
inconceivably run out of words

the curtain flaps at the window
like a sail with a broken mast
at the mercy of the wind

one
two
three
I love you
bye

I wrap myself in the sail
and sing to the compass and stars –
this litany for one voice now
because I know the words by heart
and it was your turn to hang up

turtle pond

the second-hottest day of the season
I went out to play –
left the farm chores behind
and sat in shade near my friend's pond

I envy her this pond –
surrounded by willow and alder
slightly murky, spring-fed all year

dragonflies in a palette of colors
course over the water rhythmically,
scanning for a meal

sipping root beer rickeys
after sluicing the sweat from our bodies,
we wait for the turtles to appear –
hauling out onto their platforms to sun

alpacas in the pasture
gaze in our direction curiously,
as hollyhocks nod in the garden –
almost somnolent

in the quiet heat of afternoon
space and time are stolen from a to-do list –
and sharing an affinity for drowsing turtles
our minds slow and the canvas is blank

they were a no-show after all,
probably tucked into the shady reeds,
but just counting breaths
has been enough

crossroads

before the curtain dropped
and the play was over
the actors filing back to their dressing rooms

before the ponytail was chopped off,
tied with a ribbon
and put in a blue polka-dot box

before the only way out of a maze
of wrong turns and missed chances
looked like a suitcase and a one-way ticket

no one had explained about choices –
or the not-choosing –
and the ultimate finality of both

moments of clarity, sandwiched by confusion,
sometimes arrived looking like silvan answers –
gifted from ether

fleeting flashes of intensity –
the gorget of the hummingbird,
a thrush's song echoing in the hemlock forest
or a Chopin nocturne at dawn

but drawn to the catch in the chest,
the adrenaline of risk
I chose the raft hurtling into green frothing water
and the last breath or the next
waited just below the surface

canoeing on Lake Earl

the preparation seems overwhelming at first –
until it isn't

carefully loading the canoe onto the truck
the long winding drive through redwoods

then, excitement as we arrive –
an eagle, chasing peregrines off their kill

we are not the owl and the pussycat –
but the poet and the choirmaster,

I wear periwinkle blue, you wear plum –
our sturdy cradle in the small waves

rocks to a lullaby we cannot hear
but our bodies know the tune

across the lake cattails in the swale,
elk droppings in the meadow

pussy willows on my cheek
the roar of breakers in the distance

sculpted snag skeleton in the grass –
as though arranged there

salmon and champagne, bread and orange,
a doze in the afternoon sun

the canoe, our trusted companion,
waits patiently on the shore for our return

empty mind –
we laugh and watch clouds riding the ripples

dreamscape

I am the violin and you are the desert

there used to be water and steam clouding the air
and creatures of slime held each other in the mud

but then a balloon arrived on the doorstep one day

we thought it was rubbish until it grew
and we climbed in and were wafted to the desert
where the sagebrush was a scented carpet
and tarantulas danced the tarantella

haiku for hummers

awakened early
trumpet vine opens her throat –
nectar's song seduces

shaking off torpor
hummingbird finds his solace
in the color orange

this symbiosis
of nectar, bird and pollen –
ancient archetype

fly me to the moon

the waning moon is a pale crescent
slicing daylight sky –
silent witness to this seasonal ballet –
aerialists returned to breeding ground

a swoop, a gulp, a kettle, a herd, a richness,
this flock of swallows
in their spring frenzy of pair bonding
and establishing nesting spots

soon enough the competition
for nest box real estate
begins with the bluebirds and nuthatches
looking for their own niche

somehow, disputes are settled
in time for egg laying and brood rearing
while the moon watches, imperturbable,
this familiar cadence of countless orbits

4

exclusion zone

they say the animals are thriving –
  plush and healthy after the first 6 months
  even the ones previously nearing extinction

suddenly burgeoning –
  the wolf and Przewalski's horse
  take shelter in abandoned buildings
  among overturned school desks and shattered windows

stepping over dolls and books
  left behind by bewildered children
  on a spring day in April

they are eating, sleeping, mating and giving birth –
  now without the fear of being hunted

a spider is busy spinning her web
  her appearance completely normal
  but the web just slightly off

not a perfect orb –
  but a random pattern of haphazard lines
  the only sign of something not quite right

like a kind of amnesia or dementia –
  she weaves, but has lost the architectural plans

still, scientists are amazed –
  they expected something more catastrophic
  more mutations, plummeting populations

did not expect the lush return of forest
  nor the meadows nodding with flowers

the tradeoff –
  in exchange for human predation
  irradiated, but safer – the ultimate oxymoron

in some future millennium
  constellations are winking overhead
  and Ariadne remembers her weaving

fisher

the fisher travels in the dark
   even when it is daylight

as secretive as mycelium
   creeping through the understory

as quiet as the serrated feathers
   on owl's wings

no rustle of fern or salal
   ghostlike in his blackness

a shadow easily missed
   at home in the trees

an acrobat over our heads
   when all we hear is our own footfall

almost a parallel universe –
   solitary wraith in deepest forest
even if we never see him,
   he is here, carrying his own story

we save space for the invisible –
   home ground for what is possible

P-22*

you overstepped your allotment
designated when we took over the landscape –

wandered into the backyards of
designer dogs that scamper like prey

crossed the wrong freeways –
a concrete grid overlaid on the land

meaningless, artificial boundaries
not mapped in your DNA

how could you know
only certain spaces were allowed?

how solitary your existence
far from the Santa Monica mountains

the occasional park,
a checkerboard of wild between our constructs

what happens next is our decision
as we decide everything in our dominion

your celebrity evokes some empathy,
as the wild slips away – relentless as time

P-22 was a wild mountain lion who resided in Griffith Park in Los Angeles, California

forest elk

massive and muscled,
   a white-rumped, bearded beauty
   on the cusp of rut,

he is progeny of an ancestral herd
   that knew this place –
   before the farm, before the road

when the slough ran thick with salmon,
   the forage was rich
   and egrets and heron stalked the shallows

forest of spruce and fir at his back
   he stands at the edge of a clearing
   taking in the expansive green

he has a taste for sedge and willow
   and something else –
   as yet elusive, but familiar

he lifts his head
   and bugles across the beaver meadow
   breath condensing in the chill dawn

testing the waters
   announcing his place in this world
   sending out invitations

improving the view

when I trim the overgrown viburnum
  blocking the bedroom window
  suddenly Bolan Mountain is visible
  wearing large swaths of snow and ice

it glitters white in the sun –
  bald spots where the trees were erased,
  along with the lookout over the lake,
  lost in last summer's conflagration

down the road a new neighbor from the city
  cuts down the remaining Ponderosa and fir
  overlooking the pond downhill from his house –
  to "improve" his view

someone else up the road
  removes all the conifers from the hillside –
  as if the clearcuts on the ridge were not enough –
  saying, the vista will be better up there

the remaining madrones struggle in the drought,
  suddenly without shade or screen,
  sickly, sparsely leafed and spotted
  in the relentless sun and heat of summer

ask the Steller's jays
  looking for last year's nest in the Jeffrey pine,
  ask the nuthatch
  and the pileated woodpecker

ask the great horned owl
  who took his daytime drowse
  in the ancient sugar pine facing Bolan Mountain
  and waited for dusk

ask the tall ones who cannot run
  whose voices cannot be heard
  who message each other, underground,
  in a language we have not learned

ask them about the new improved views –
  they will not answer –
  the asking is only a gentle zephyr
  soughing through the canopy of the missing

descent

the nuthatch flits from persimmon to redbud
plucks pieces of bark from one

disappears into the hollowed trunk of another
this descent into the dark a welcoming

familiar and safe – the site of last year's nest –
he is sure of another season, another brood

half a world away the gathered fallen
lie in trenches

embraced by the soil of home
the darkest silence unimagined

like the bird that strikes the window
their final descent unreckoned

we listen for a song in the smoky wind
but no birds remain in Mariupol

telling the bees

the spring dried up in this drought year
and I hung an indigo ribbon over the source,
offered a brief whispered incantation
and then went to tell the bees

tradition dictates all major events
must be shared with the bees
and a shroud must be placed over the hive
at the news of a death

I wanted to find some good news
to balance out the incendiary summer,
but then the unthinkable happened –
the hives melted in the relentless heat

there was frenzy –
workers looking for their queen –
without her there would be no brood
and the hive would die

honey and wax pooled on the grass –
an ant discovered the bounty
and soon others began arriving
like a choreographed chorus line

when we weren't paying attention
our planet started handing out eviction notices
and there is no grace period any more
and I'm still looking for a shroud

the verge

between the clearcut and the creek
or the pasture and the pavement
lie unruly ribbons of land
bordered by a verge

a wild vestige – by design or accident –
harboring rusted hulks and plastic detritus
these forgotten spaces rich with life
of no particular use to anyone

where a seed falls at random and germinates
and no one notices or cares
the wren nests in a truck's shell
and the banana slug humbly creates humus

when the farms lie idle, the cities abandoned,
and the highways are silent,
the verge holds the secret of returning –
nudges the land into reclamation

grass grows in the cracks in the asphalt,
a jigsaw puzzle of green and grey,
redwood and cedar sprout in the lumber yard
nourished by the sawdust of their ancestors

elk browse the last of summer's roses
along the overgrown hedgerows
near the farm house moldering into the loam,
ivy overtaking the porch railings

as Charon collects the last of his silver coins
from the eyelids of humanity
a bear and her yearling cubs
loll in the window frames and doorways

blinking in the sun breaking through the fog
they breathe the new green quiet
as though they always have
and listen to the verge inching forward

sharp-shinned

the finches are yellow ornaments
decorating the leafless persimmon of winter
until they suddenly shatter

into the shelter of the rosemary and hebe,
as a sharp-shinned hawk swoops
and lands in the cottonwoods

biding his time, he preens for 20 minutes,
occasionally lifts his head to scan the field
where snow still lies in patches

then swivels to face the garden
where fruit tree prunings are piled,
looking like beaver dams waiting for water

he flicks his white-banded tail
while songbirds huddle, waiting him out –
the feeders hanging solitary and abandoned

in the morning I find downy gray feathers,
softer than breath, with droplets of dew
mirroring the sky they once inhabited

as I refill feeders with nuts and seeds
to soften winter's indifferent tyranny
the hawk does not go hungry

the healer's hands

the healer's hands work with clay now –
hands intimate with the chronic,
the congenital or the skeletal
hands that cradled newborns
or brushed the shoulder of the elderly
while offering reassurances
or the brutal honesty
of a hopeless diagnosis

no one knows better
that flesh is so unpredictable
and decomposition – inevitable

as he forms and molds –
the clay supple and forgiving
the shaping satisfying and sensual
hands sculpt in a reciprocal rhythm
until the glazing and surrender to the kiln –
the shimmer skin of preservation –
not mending, but a kind of birthing
finally – the perfect vessel

sparing the mandrake

healer
witch
crone
take your pick –
the centuries are fickle
when it comes to belief

lush, rampant untidiness beckons –
comfrey and wormwood
echinacea and valerian

hang the bundles to dry,
infuse the berries in alcohol –
tincture and tonic
infusion and balm

half gallon jars set in the sun,
purple and scarlet jewels
set amongst the rosemary and poppies

clean the smaller tinted bottles
discarded a century ago
along the muddy bank
near the homestead spring

                *

something must always remain –
the last apple on the tree
the last currants on the bush
the last ear of corn
a kind of gratitude

in this case,
I find the mandrake, sturdily rooted
and smiling, I leave him there
safe from the scream
superstition speaks of – just in case

we have a shared sensibility –
he only wants this earthen hiding place,
damp and secluded
preferring solitude – oblivious to omen

chrysalis

the swallowtail chrysalis startles me
   in the midst of pruning the fruit trees

emerald green, it looks like a jewel
   attached to a gray twig of the fig tree
   with two silken strands – guy wires

fine enough to thread a needle –
   impossibly precarious and fragile
   in this snow and sleet of March

as precarious as the deer
   venturing down out of the woods
   wading belly deep through snow

as one, a pregnant doe, separates herself
   to scrape at the snow and finds the winter squash
   we left under the Jeffrey pine

as precarious as the hummingbirds
   coming out of torpor in early morning
   to find their feeders

having survived another night
   under a flake of bark or
   in a crevice of siding under the overhang

as precarious as our world
   of mass shootings, road rage and wars
   and we who survive call ourselves…*lucky*

no sugar water, squash nor hand-wringing
   can help this chrysalis
   who waits – patient and resolute

for the warm summer day
   when she unfurls her black and yellow wings
   to dry in the sun

sure of her season, emergence may take hours or days –
   is it struggle or bliss?

 if I happen to be watching – astonished –
 I will call her…*resilient*
 and I will call myself…*lucky*

acknowledgements

Grateful acknowledgement is made to the editors of the following publications in which some of these poems (sometimes in different versions) first appeared or are forthcoming:

Canary (story in the stone, the verge)
Cirque (shapeshifting, waking)
Eunoia Review (canoeing on lake earl. chrysalis, fisher, forest elk, improving the view, ode to old uprights, reading the stars)
Fireweed (muscle tree)
New Verse New (P-22)
Otoliths (cypher)
Pedestal Magazine (cephalopod)
Takilma Common Ground (winter grace)
Turtle Island Quarterly (an exuberant shout, cantabile, duff, feral, from the sea, telling the bees, winesap)

about the author

Barbara Parchim is a poet, gardener, nature enthusiast, visual artist, and frequent wildlife rehabber. She owns and works an organic farm in Oregon that was originally homesteaded in the late 1800s. From an early age she was drawn to the natural world as a place of refuge and discovery and has drawn inspiration and solace from her interactions with wildlife and nature. As a visual artist, Barbara enjoys integrating her writing with her visual imagery. She has worked variously as a landscaper, nursery worker, apple picker, library assistant, travel agent and social worker and volunteered for several years at a wildlife rehab and education center caring for resident raptors and wolves. Her first book of poetry, *What Remains*, was published by Flowstone Press in October, 2021.

www.ingramcontent.com/pod-product-compliance
Lightning Source LLC
Chambersburg PA
CBHW060538080526
44586CB00012B/779